127 HOBBIES FOR ALPHA MEN

(The Best Manly Ideas To Have Fun, Despite Your Wife)

THE ALPHA MAN

Let's be honest for a second. Men are not perfect. We need some space sometimes.

I am not gonna deny what they say about us: we are childioh sometimes, we are simple, we don't always have something to say.

But think for a minute how this world would be without us, men, the alphas.

There would be no wars but there would be a lot of crying, a lot of hugging, a lot of talking about feelings.

This book is for all the alphas out there who sometimes need to escape their homes and wives and children and do something for themselves.

Here you will find 127 hobbies that will make you feel like a real man again.

From the simple (but essential) things like motorcycling and drinking your own beer, to the more adventurous ones like river rafting and flying.

So what are you waiting for? Get out there and start living your life to the fullest!

The Alpha Man
(a simple guy just like you who doesn't have the guts to publish this book without a pseudonym)

CONTENTS

AIRSOFT

Airsoft is a great hobby for men who want to feel like they're in an action movie. It's a competitive sport that requires skill, strategy, and teamwork. Plus, it's a great way to blow off some steam and relieve stress.

Airsoft is also a great way to bond with friends and family. You can spend hours together playing in the woods or in your backyard, and it's a great way to stay active. And, of course, it's always more fun to shoot at someone when you know they're not going to shoot back.

So, if you're looking for a hobby that's masculine, challenging, and fun, look no further than airsoft. Just be sure to leave the women and children at home.

ALCOHOL CONNOISSEUR

There's nothing better than kicking back with a cold beer after a long day. But why settle for just any old beer when you can explore the world of craft beer and become an alcohol connoisseur?

Benefits of this hobby include:

1. Tasting different beers and learning to appreciate the subtle differences in flavor.

2. Meeting like-minded people and sharing your passion with others.

3. Getting to know your local breweries and supporting their efforts.

4. Becoming a more knowledgeable and well-rounded drinker.

So crack open a cold one and start your journey to becoming an alcohol connoisseur today!

AMATEUR ASTRONOMY

There's nothing like spending a clear night out in the middle of nowhere, away from the light pollution of the city, to get a really good look at the stars. And there's nothing quite like amateur astronomy to give you a newfound appreciation for just how big and empty the universe is.

Sure, your wife might think you're a little crazy for spending all night looking at the stars, but she doesn't understand the joys of amateur astronomy. And your kids will probably never appreciate how cool it is to be able to find the constellations in the night sky. But that's okay, because amateur astronomy is a hobby that's really for you, not them.

So go ahead and set up your telescope in the backyard and spend your nights stargazing. It's a great way to relax, unwind, and appreciate the universe we live in.

ANALOG GAMES

Analog games are the best way to spend your free time - especially if you want to avoid your nagging wife or screaming kids. There's something satisfying about unplugging from the digital world and playing a game that doesn't require batteries.

Plus, analog games are great for your brain. They help improve your critical thinking skills and problem-solving abilities. And unlike video games, you can't just turn them off when you get frustrated - you have to finish what you started, no matter how long it takes. That's character-building stuff, right there.

So if you're looking for a hobby that's both fun and beneficial, look no further than analog games. And if your wife or kids give you grief about it, just tell them you're preparing for the zombie apocalypse. They'll leave you alone real quick.

ANIMAL RESCUING

There's nothing more manly than rescuing a helpless animal. It's like killing two birds with one stone: you get to feel like a badass while also helping out a poor, defenseless creature. Plus, it's a great way to meet women. Just tell them you're a big, strong man who rescues animals and they'll be swooning all over you.

Benefits of animal rescuing include:

-You get to feel like a hero

-You get to meet cute animals

-You get to meet potential romantic partners who appreciate your kind heart

So what are you waiting for? Get out there and start rescuing some animals!

ANTIQUING

There's nothing like the thrill of the hunt when you're out antiquing. It's the perfect way to spend a lazy Sunday afternoon, combing through musty old stores in search of that hidden gem. And when you finally find it, the feeling is unbeatable.

Not only is antiquing a great way to score some unique and interesting pieces for your home, it's also a great way to get out and about and explore your local community. Plus, it's a great way to bond with yoursignificant other or friends.

So next time you're feeling bored and restless, why not try your hand at antiquing? You might just find yourself hooked.

ARCHERY

Archery is a great hobby for men. It's a great way to relieve stress, get some exercise, and spend time outdoors. Plus, it's a great way to show off your manly skills.

Archery is also a great way to teach your children the value of discipline and focus. If you can teach them to hit the target, they can learn to hit their goals in life.

And, of course, archery is a great way to impress the ladies. There's nothing sexier than a man who can shoot a bow and arrow with precision. So, if you're looking for a way to score some points with the fairer sex, take up archery.

BACKPACKING

Backpacking is a great way to get away from the hustle and bustle of everyday life. It's a chance to explore the great outdoors, and to get some exercise while you're at it. Plus, it's a great way to meet new people and see new places.

There are many benefits to backpacking, but here are just a few:

1. It's great exercise. Hiking up mountains and carrying a heavy backpack is a great workout.

2. It's a great way to see the world. When you backpack, you can really get off the beaten path and see some amazing places that most people never get to see.

3. It's a great way to meet new people. When you travel, you meet all sorts of interesting people from all over the world.

4. It's a great way to get away from it all. If you're feeling stressed out or just need a break from the grind, backpacking is the perfect way to reset and recharge.

5. It's a great way to connect with nature. When you're out in the wilderness, you can't help but appreciate the beauty of nature.

If you're looking for a hobby that is both exciting and beneficial, look no further than backpacking. It's the perfect way to get away from the everyday and experience something new.

BALLROOM DANCING

There's nothing like the thrill of gliding across the dance floor, your feet moving in perfect unison with your partner's. But when your partner is your wife, it can sometimes feel more like a chore than a hobby.

Still, there's something to be said for the discipline and artistry of ballroom dancing. It's a great way to get some exercise, and it's a lot more fun than mowing the lawn.

So if you're looking for a way to impress your wife or girlfriend, or if you just want to learn something new, give ballroom dancing a try. Just be prepared to be laughed at by your friends.

BARBECUING

Barbecuing is the perfect hobby for any red-blooded, All-American male. It combines the three things we love most: meat, fire, and making women do all the work.

What's not to love about barbecuing? You get to fire up a big grill, throw some meat on it, and sit back with a cold beer while your wife or girlfriend does all the work. And if she complains, you can always tell her that "the way to a man's heart is through his stomach."

Seriously, what's not to love about barbecuing? It's the perfect way to spend a summer afternoon. So fire up the grill and invite your friends over for some burgers and beers. And don't forget to invite your wife or girlfriend – she can bring the salad.

BEARD GROOMING

There's nothing more manly than taking care of your beard. It's like a symbol of virility and power. Plus, it keeps your face warm in the winter and protects you from the sun in the summer. But more than that, it's a way to show the world that you're a real man.

Beard grooming is an important part of any man's hygiene routine. It's not just about looking good – although that's certainly a benefit. It's also about keeping your beard healthy and free of debris.

There are a few key things you need to do to groom your beard properly. First, you need to wash it regularly with a mild shampoo. Second, you need to comb it out to remove tangles and knots. Third, you need to trim it regularly to keep it looking neat and tidy.

The benefits of beard grooming are numerous. Not only does it make you look more handsome, but it also keeps your beard healthy and free of debris. Plus, it's a great way to show the world that you're a real man. So go ahead and take pride in your beard – it's well deserved.

BEEKEEPING

There are few hobbies as manly as beekeeping. First of all, you get to wear a cool suit and smoke a smoker (which, let's be honest, is just an excuse to light something on fire). Plus, you get to work with deadly creatures and handle large amounts of honey (the nectar of the gods). And what could be more satisfying than turning the sweet, sticky labor of bees into delicious honey that you can eat or sell?

Not only is beekeeping a manly hobby, it's also a useful one. Honey is a natural antiseptic and can be used to treat wounds. It's also a great cough suppressant and can be used to make mead, a delicious alcoholic beverage. Plus, bees are responsible for pollinating a third of the world's crops, so by keeping bees you're helping to ensure a food supply for the world.

So not only is beekeeping manly, it's also heroic.

BEER BREWING

Brewing beer is the perfect hobby for any self-respecting man. It's a manly pursuit that requires patience, skill and a willingness to get your hands dirty. Plus, it's a great way to impress your friends and family.

There are few things more satisfying than cracking open a cold one that you've brewed yourself. And the best part is, it's not nearly as difficult as you might think. With a little practice, you can be brewing beer that's just as good as anything you'd find at your local pub.

So what are you waiting for? Grab some friends, fire up the grill and get brewing!

BILLIARDS

There's nothing like sinking a few balls into a pocket to help you forget your troubles. And what better way to do it than with a game of billiards?

This masculine hobby is the perfect way to spend an evening with your buddies, drinking beer and smoking cigars. And if you're lucky, you might even get to see a fight break out.

Benefits of playing billiards include improving your hand-eye coordination, sharpening your focus, and increasing your level of concentration. Plus, it's a great way to relieve stress and tension.

So if you're looking for a way to unwind and have some fun, grab a cue stick and challenge your friends to a game of billiards. Just make sure you don't let your wife catch you, or she'll have your hide.

BLOGGING

Blogging is the best hobby for any man who wants to feel like he's the most important person in the world. It's a great way to spend some time each day pontificating on whatever topics happen to be on your mind, and it's a great way to build up an audience of adoring fans who will agree with everything you say.

Plus, it's a great way to procrastinate on actually doing anything productive. Why work on that project you've been meaning to get to when you can just spend an hour writing a blog post about how you're going to get to it?

And of course, there's the added bonus of being able to annoy your wife or girlfriend with constant updates on your latest blog post, or by using your blog as a platform to complain about how she's nagging you to do something around the house.

So if you're looking for a hobby that will make you feel important, give you an outlet for your opinions, and help you procrastinate on actually doing anything, then blogging is the perfect hobby for you.

BONSAI TREES

Bonsai trees are a great hobby for men who want to feel like they're in control of something. After all, what could be more manly than carefully shaping a tree to your will? It's a great way to assert your dominance over nature.

Plus, bonsai trees are a great way to annoy your wife or girlfriend. If she's constantly nagging you to do something around the house, just tell her you're busy working on your bonsai tree and she'll leave you alone. Trust me, it works like a charm.

And if you have kids, bonsai trees are a great way to get them to stop bugging you. Just tell them you're busy shaping your tree and they'll leave you alone. It's the perfect way to get some peace and quiet.

BOWLING

Bowling is a great hobby for men. It's a sport that requires skill, accuracy, and precision. It's also a sport that is a great way to relieve stress. And, it's a great way to socialize with other men.

Bowling is a great way to spend some time with your buddies. It's a way to bond over some friendly competition. And, it's a great way to blow off some steam.

Bowling is also a great way to stay in shape. It's a physical activity that gets your heart rate up and gets you moving. It's also a great way to burn some calories.

So, if you're looking for a hobby that is masculine, challenging, and fun, then bowling is the perfect activity for you.

BOXING

There's nothing like a good boxing match. Two men in a ring, throwing punches at each other until one is knocked out. It's a sport of true men.

And what's even better than watching a boxing match? Participating in one. There's nothing like the feeling of your fist connecting with your opponent's face. It's the ultimate way to relieve stress.

Not to mention, it's great exercise. You'll be toning your arms and shoulders, and getting a cardio workout at the same time. And if you're lucky, you might even get a black eye or two. What's not to love?

So if you're looking for a hobby that's both manly and fun, look no further than boxing. Trust me, you won't regret it.

BICYCLING

There's nothing like the feeling of the wind in your hair as you zoom down the open road on your bicycle. It's the perfect way to clear your head and get some exercise. Plus, it's a great way to annoy your wife by pedaling faster than she can walk.

BIRDING

There's nothing more manly than getting up before the sun to go birding. You get to be outside in nature, communing with the birds. And there's nothing more satisfying than spotting a rare bird and ticking it off your list.

Benefits of birding include:

- Fresh air

- Exercise

- Quiet time to think

- bragging rights over your birding buddies

- an excuse to buy expensive binoculars and other gear

So get out there and start birding! And if your wife/girlfriend/kids complain, just tell them you're doing your manly duty.

CAMPING

There are few things more manly than heading into the great outdoors for a weekend of camping. There's something about being out in nature, away from the hustle and bustle of everyday life, that just makes a man feel more alive. Plus, it's a great opportunity to get away from nagging wives and screaming kids.

Camping is a great way to unwind and relax. It's also a great way to bond with friends and family. There's nothing like sitting around the campfire, sharing stories and laughing together. And of course, there's the added bonus of being able to enjoy the peace and quiet of nature.

So if you're looking for a great way to relax, bond with friends and family, and escape the stresses of everyday life, then camping is the perfect hobby for you.

CANOEING

There's nothing quite like canoeing to get away from it all - especially if you're trying to get away from your nagging wife. Just hop in your canoe and paddle away from all her screaming.

Of course, canoeing isn't just a great way to escape your wife. It's also a great way to get some exercise and enjoy the great outdoors. And what could be more manly than that?

So get out there and enjoy some canoeing - just make sure you leave your wife at home.

CAR RACING

Car racing is the perfect hobby for any real man. It's fast, it's dangerous, and it's really, really loud. Plus, you get to wear cool helmets and drive really expensive cars.

There are few things in life that are more exhilarating than strapping yourself into a high-powered machine and hurtling around a track at breakneck speeds. And when you're done, you can brag to your buddies about how you smoked them on the straightaway.

Car racing is also a great way to relieve stress. After a long day at work, there's nothing like getting behind the wheel and letting loose. You can forget all your troubles and just focus on the task at hand: going as fast as humanly possible.

So if you're looking for a hobby that's exciting, manly, and just a little bit dangerous, car racing is the perfect activity for you.

CARD GAMES

Card games are a great way to pass the time, whether you're by yourself or with a group of friends. They can be a fun way to relieve stress, and they can also be a great way to socialize and make new friends.

Some of the benefits of playing card games include:

-They're a great way to kill time

-They can help relieve stress

-They're a great way to socialize and make new friends

-They can be a lot of fun

So, if you're looking for a way to pass the time, relieve some stress, or just have some fun, grab a deck of cards and give them a try.

CIGARS

Cigars are a great way to relax and enjoy yourself. They're perfect for enjoying after a meal, or while you're out on the town. They're also a great conversation starter, and a great way to bond with other cigar aficionados.

Cigars are also a great way to show off your wealth and status. They're a luxurious item that not everyone can afford, so smoking a cigar is a great way to show that you're doing well for yourself.

Finally, cigars are just plain manly. There's something about the act of smoking a cigar that just oozes masculinity. If you're looking for a hobby that will make you feel more like a man, then smoking cigars is definitely the way to go.

Of course, be careful: smoking is not the best idea for a longer life.

CLASSIC CAR RESTORATION

There's nothing like the feeling of taking an old, rusty classic car and restoring it to its former glory. It's a labor of love, and it's also a great way to piss off your wife. Every time she asks you to do something around the house, you can just tell her that you're too busy working on the car. It's a win-win!

COACH A KIDS TEAM

Coaching a kids' team is a great way to get away from the nagging wife. It's a chance to be a leader and impart your wisdom on the young'uns. Plus, you get to relive your glory days on the field/court/etc. And, if the team does well, you get to brag to all the other parents about how great of a coach you are.

COFFEE ROASTING

Coffee roasting is a great hobby for men. It's a way to relax and enjoy the process of making your own coffee. Plus, it's a great way to impress your friends and family with your mad coffee roasting skills.

There are many benefits to coffee roasting, including the fact that you can control the quality of your coffee, the strength of the flavor, and the level of caffeine. Plus, it's a great way to save money on your coffee habit.

So if you're looking for a masculine hobby that will relax you and impress your friends, look no further than coffee roasting.

COLLECTING

There's something special about the feeling of acquiring a new piece for your collection. Whether it's a new comic book, a limited edition action figure, or a vintage record, the sense of satisfaction that comes with adding to your collection is unlike any other.

For some, collecting is simply a fun hobby, a way to pass the time. But for others, it's a way of life. Collectors take great pride in their collections, and for good reason. Not only does collecting require knowledge and passion, but it also takes dedication and discipline.

There are many benefits to collecting, both mental and physical. Collecting can help relieve stress, boost your mood, and improve your memory. It can also help you make new friends and connections, and can even lead to new career opportunities.

But perhaps the most important benefit of collecting is the simple joy it brings. There's something special about surrounding yourself with things you love. So if you're looking for a hobby that's both fun and rewarding, look no further than collecting.

COMPUTER PROGRAMMING

There's nothing quite like the feeling of accomplishment you get after writing a line of code that actually works. And it's even better when that code is actually useful, like when you build a program that can automatically generate grocery lists based on what's already in your pantry.

Sure, some people might say that computer programming is a nerdy hobby, but we know that it's really the ultimate form of manliness. After all, what could be more masculine than using your brain to create something tangible and useful?

And unlike some other hobbies, computer programming is actually useful in the real world. In today's economy, being able to code is becoming increasingly valuable, and it's a skill that can be used to make some serious money.

So if you're looking for a hobby that will make you feel like a real man, look no further than computer programming.

COOKING

Most of the world known chefs are men. Is it a coincidence?

Nah.

It takes a real man to cook. It's not just about throwing some meat on the grill, it's an art. It's a way to show your creative side, and your prowess in the kitchen. Plus, it's a great way to get laid.

There's nothing that women love more than a man who can cook. It's like a secret weapon. You can cook her dinner, and then afterwards she'll be so grateful that she'll probably put out. And if she doesn't, you can always hold it over her head. "If you don't put out, I'm not going to cook for you anymore." That'll show her who's boss.

Plus, it's a great way to impress your friends. They'll be like, "Whoa, this guy can cook? He's a total badass." And then they'll be jealous of your mad skills.

So if you're looking for a hobby that's manly, creative, and will get you laid, then cooking is the way to go.

CROSSWORD PUZZLES

Crossword puzzles are the perfect way to while away a few hours on a rainy day. They're also a great way to make yourself feel superior to your wife/girlfriend/child, who will no doubt be struggling to complete even the easiest of clues.

The benefits of this hobby are numerous. Not only will you get a smug sense of satisfaction from being able to complete the puzzle with ease, you'll also improve your vocabulary and problem-solving skills. And, if you're really lucky, you might even find a clue that makes you laugh out loud.

CURRENCY COLLECTING

Currency collecting is a great hobby for men. It's a way to show your masculinity and your knowledge of the world. It's also a great way to make some extra money.

The benefits of currency collecting are many. First, it's a great way to learn about different countries and their cultures. Second, it's a great way to make some extra money. Third, it's a great way to impress your friends and family. Fourth, it's a great way to get out of the house and meet new people.

So, if you're looking for a great hobby that will make you some extra money,currency collecting is the hobby for you!

DARTS

Darts is a great hobby for men. It's a masculine activity that requires skill and precision. It's also a great way to relieve stress and blow off some steam.

There are many benefits to playing darts. It's a great way to socialize with other men, and it's also a great way to improve your hand-eye coordination. Plus, it's a lot of fun.

If you're looking for a great way to spend some time with your buddies, or if you're just looking for a new hobby, darts is a great option.

DRAWING AND PAINTING

Drawing and painting is a great hobby for men. It's a great way to relax, and it's a great way to express your creative side. Plus, it's a great way to make your wife and kids happy. After all, what woman doesn't want a man who can draw and paint?

Seriously though, drawing and painting is a great hobby for anyone. It's a great way to relieve stress, and it's a great way to express yourself. Whether you're a man or a woman, drawing and painting is a great way to unwind and have some fun.

DRAWING / WRITING COMIC STRIPS

Drawing comic strips is a great way to procrastinate. It's also a great way to make your wife and children laugh. And, if you're lucky, you might even make a few bucks off of it.

DOG TRAINING

The benefits of dog training are many and varied.

It's a great way to impress your friends and intimidate your enemies. And of course, there's the satisfaction that comes from knowing that you've taken a wild animal and turned it into a obedient tool of destruction.

So if you're looking for a hobby that's both manly and fun, dog training is the way to go. Just be sure to keep your wife and kids away from the dogs when they're in training mode.

FALCONRY

There's nothing like spending a beautiful day outdoors with your loyal bird of prey by your side. Falconry is the perfect hobby for those who appreciate the finer things in life, like spending hours training your bird and then watching it soar through the sky.

Benefits of falconry include getting to spend time outdoors, bonding with your bird, and impressing your friends and family with your skills. Not to mention, it's a great way to get some exercise. And let's be honest, there's nothing more satisfying than watching your bird take down a hapless animal.

So if you're looking for a hobby that's both challenging and rewarding, look no further than falconry. Just be sure to set aside plenty of time for it, as it's not something you can half-ass and still expect to be successful at.

FANTASY SPORTS

Fantasy sports is the perfect hobby for any self-respecting man. It combines the excitement of sports with the satisfaction of winning money off your friends.

Plus, it's a great way to procrastinate at work or avoid spending time with your family. If you're looking for an excuse to stay up all night drinking beer and arguing with strangers, fantasy sports is for you!

FENCING

Fencing is a great hobby for men. It's a sport that requires skill, athleticism, and strategy. It's also a sport that is often misunderstood. People often think that fencing is simply two people waving swords at each other, but there is so much more to it than that.

Fencing is a great way to get exercise. It's a full-body workout that gets your heart pumping and your muscles working. It's also a great way to blow off some steam. Fencing is a very intense sport, and sometimes it can be quite frustrating. But it's also extremely satisfying to score a touch against your opponent.

Fencing is also a great way to meet new people. If you join a fencing club, you'll quickly make new friends who share your passion for the sport. You'll also get to meet people from all walks of life, which can be very enriching.

So if you're looking for a hobby that is challenging, rewarding, and fun, look no further than fencing. It's the perfect activity for any man who wants to feel like a true Renaissance warrior.

FISHING

Fishing is one of the most manly hobbies out there. It requires patience, skill, and a whole lot of manly know-how. Plus, it's a great way to get away from the nagging wife and screaming kids.

There's nothing quite like spending a peaceful day out on the water, surrounded by nature, waiting for that big catch. And when you finally land it, there's no feeling quite like it. It's a great way to relax, unwind, and clear your head.

Plus, fishing is a great way to get some exercise. You'll be out in the fresh air, getting some sun, and getting your heart rate up as you reel in those big fish.

So if you're looking for a hobby that's relaxing, manly, and a whole lot of fun, then look no further than fishing.

FLYING

There's nothing quite like the feeling of taking to the skies in a small aircraft. It's just you, the wind in your hair, and the vast open sky. It's the ultimate in freedom.

And what's not to love about spending hundreds of dollars an hour to fly around in a metal death trap? It's exhilarating, it's manly, and it's a great way to impress the ladies.

Seriously though, there's something about flying that just gets the blood pumping. It's the perfect way to blow off some steam after a long week at work. And there's nothing like the satisfaction of landing a plane safely after a long flight.

So if you're looking for a hobby that's both exciting and manly, look no further than flying. Just be sure to keep your wife and kids far away from the airport.

FLYING DRONES

Drone flying is a great hobby for any man who wants to feel like a kid again. It's a great way to blow off some steam and forget about your problems for a while. Plus, it's a great way to annoy your wife or children. They'll never know what hit them when you start buzzing them with your drone.

FOOTBALL

Football is the ultimate masculine sport. It requires strength, speed, and agility. It is a sport that requires split-second decisions and relies on teamwork. Football is a sport that instills discipline and requires dedication and commitment. Football is a sport that teaches young men how to be leaders and how to work together for a common goal. Football is a sport that builds character and teaches young men how to handle adversity. Football is the ultimate masculine sport.

GARDENING

Gardening is a great hobby for men. It's a great way to get some exercise, get some fresh air, and to get away from the nagging wife. Plus, you can grow your own food and save money on groceries.

There's nothing better than a freshly grown tomato or cucumber. And you can grow them as big as you want. Just make sure to keep an eye on the wife - she'll probably try to steal them for her salad.

GENEALOGY

There's nothing more manly than delving into your family history. It's a way to connect with your roots, learn about where you come from, and give yourself a sense of identity. And what could be more satisfying than unearthing some juicy scandal or long-lost relative?

Sure, your wife might give you grief about spending hours poring over dusty old records. And your kids might roll their eyes when you regale them with stories of your great-great-grandfather's exploits. But who cares? You're a man on a mission, and nothing's going to stop you from finding out who your ancestors were and what made them tick.

GEOCACHING

Geocaching is a real-world, outdoor treasure hunting game using GPS-enabled devices. Participants navigate to a specific set of GPS coordinates and then attempt to find the geocache (container) hidden at that location.

Benefits of geocaching includes getting some fresh air and exercise, spending time with family and friends, and exploring new places. It's a great way to get out of the house and have some fun!

Some people like to complain that geocaching is a waste of time, but they're just jealous because they're not the ones finding all the cool stuff. So, if you're looking for a fun way to get out and about, try your hand at geocaching!

GHOST TOWNS EXPLORATION

There's something uniquely satisfying about exploring a ghost town. Maybe it's the feeling of stepping back in time, or the sense of being somewhere that's been abandoned by civilization. Whatever the reason, there's something special about these places.

And the best part is that they're all over the country, just waiting to be explored. So whether you're looking for a weekend getaway or a longer adventure, there's sure to be a ghost town that's perfect for you.

So what are you waiting for? Pack your bags and hit the road – the ghost towns are calling!

GLASS-BLOWING

There's nothing like the sound of a woman's screams when you're blowing glass. It's like music to my ears. Plus, it's a great way to release some pent-up aggression.

Glass-blowing is a great way to relax and unwind after a long day. It's also a great way to impress your friends and family. And, if you're really good at it, you can even make some money on the side.

GO-KARTING

There's nothing quite like the thrill of zipping around a track at high speeds in a tiny go-kart. It's the perfect way to blow off some steam and forget about the mundane realities of life. Plus, it's a great way to impress the ladies.

Not only is go-karting insanely fun, it also has a few benefits. For one, it's an excellent way to improve your driving skills. And let's be honest, who doesn't want to be a better driver? It's also a great way to stay in shape, as it requires a fair amount of upper body strength to steer a go-kart around a track.

So if you're looking for a fun hobby that will also give you a few benefits, go-karting is the way to go. Just be sure to wear a helmet, because things can get pretty dangerous out there on the track.

GOLF

Golf is a great hobby for men. It's a great way to get outdoors, get some exercise, and spend time with friends. Golf is also a great way to relieve stress and clear your head. And, let's be honest, it's a great way to impress your boss or clients. Golf is a game of skill, strategy, and concentration. It's a game that requires patience and practice. But, it's a game that's worth it. Golf is a great way to spend a day, a weekend, or a lifetime.

GRAPHIC DESIGN

Graphic design is a great hobby for any man. It allows you to be creative, and to express yourself in a unique way. Plus, it's a great way to procrastinate from doing actual work.

Benefits of graphic design include:

- You can make yourself look more attractive to women, by creating a nice portfolio.

- You can make money by doing freelance work, or even start your own design business.

- You can annoy your wife or girlfriend by constantly talking about design theory, and showing her your latest creations.

- You can spend hours upon hours staring at a screen, and not get bored.

So if you're looking for a hobby that is both creative and manly, look no further than graphic design!

HAM RADIO

Ham radio is the perfect hobby for any man who wants to escape the nagging of his wife, the screaming of his kids, and the general chaos of daily life. With ham radio, you can tune into any conversation you want, anywhere in the world, and no one can tell you to stop or change the channel. It's the perfect way to relax and unwind after a long day.

HAMMOCKING

Hammocking is the perfect way to relax and take a nap without having to worry about your wife or kids bothering you. It's like having your own personal oasis. Plus, it's a great way to get some fresh air and Vitamin D.

HAVING SEX

Having sex is one of the most enjoyable hobbies a man can have. It's a great way to relieve stress, burn calories, and just have plain old fun. And, unlike other hobbies, it's something you can do with your wife or girlfriend (or both!).

There are many benefits to having sex. For one, it's a great way to burn calories. In fact, you can burn up to 200 calories in just 30 minutes. That's the same as running at a 6-minute mile pace! And, if you're looking to lose weight, sex is a great way to help. In addition to burning calories, sex also helps you to sleep better, reduces stress, and can boost your immune system.

So, what are you waiting for? Get out there and have some fun!

HIKING

Hiking is a great way to get some exercise and fresh air. It's also a great way to clear your head and get away from the grind of everyday life.

There are plenty of benefits to hiking, including getting some fresh air and exercise, clearing your head, and spending time in nature. But one of the best things about hiking is that it's a great way to get away from your nagging wife or screaming kids.

So next time you're feeling stressed out, ditch the rat race and head for the hills. It's the perfect way to recharge your batteries and get some peace and quiet.

HISTORICAL REENACTMENT

There's nothing quite like historical reenactment to get you in touch with your inner man. There's something about donning a period costume and stepping back in time that just makes you feel more virile. And what could be more manly than recreating famous battles or acts of heroism?

Not only is historical reenactment a great way to get in touch with your inner man, but it also has a number of other benefits. For one, it's a great way to stay in shape. After all, those old-timey costumes can be quite constricting, and lugging around all that heavy equipment is no easy feat.

Additionally, historical reenactment is a great way to learn about history. What better way to learn about the American Revolution than by putting on a red coat and marching around with a musket? You can also learn a lot about strategy and tactics by watching other reenactors in action.

So if you're looking for a hobby that will make you feel more manly, help you stay in shape, and teach you a thing or two about history, look no further than historical reenactment.

HOME PROJECTS

There's nothing better than coming home after a long day at work and starting a nice, big home project. It's a great way to blow off some steam and really get your hands dirty. Plus, it's a great way to procrastinate on doing things that you actually have to do, like cleaning the house or spending time with your family.

The benefits of home projects are numerous. For one, it gives you a sense of accomplishment when you finally finish that long-awaited task. It also saves you a ton of money, since you're doing the work yourself instead of hiring someone else to do it. And let's not forget the most important benefit: it gives you something to talk to your friends about at the next barbeque. "Oh, you're having trouble with your sink? I just fixed my leaky toilet last weekend. Let me tell you all about it."

HORSEBACK RIDING

Horseback riding is a great hobby for men. It's a great way to get some exercise, fresh air, and to feel like a real man. There's nothing like saddling up a horse and riding off into the sunset. Plus, it's a great way to meet women. What could be more romantic than a man on a horse? Just be careful that your horse doesn't get too excited when you're around women.

INVESTING MONEY

There's nothing quite like the feeling of making money from investing. It's a rush like no other. And the best part is, you can do it in your spare time!

Investing is a great way to make your money work for you. With a little research and some careful planning, you can earn a healthy return on your investment without putting in a lot of work.

Plus, investing is a great way to diversify your income streams. If you have a portfolio of investments, you'll be less likely to feel the pinch if one of your income sources dries up.

So if you're looking for a way to make some extra cash, invest in yourself and start earning from your investments today!

JOINING THE FREEMASONS

The Freemasons are a brotherhood of men committed to making the world a better place. They meet regularly to help each other grow in wisdom and strength, and to support each other in our endeavors. Freemasonry is a great way to meet new friends and to network with like-minded men. And, of course, the Freemasons are always ready to lend a helping hand to those in need.

JOURNALING

Journaling is a great way to get your thoughts and feelings down on paper. It can be a therapeutic way to release stress and work through your problems.Journaling can also be a great way to document your life and experiences. You can look back on your journal entries and reflect on your life, your growth, and your journey.

KNIFE THROWING

There's nothing quite like the satisfaction of throwing a knife and hearing it stick into the target with a satisfying thunk. Knife throwing is a great hobby for anyone looking to relieve some stress, or just have some fun.

Plus, it's a great way to impress your friends and family. Just imagine their reactions when you pull out a knife and start throwing it around like a pro!

Benefits of knife throwing include improved hand-eye coordination, increased focus, and improved motor skills. Not to mention, it's just really satisfying to stick a knife into a target.

So if you're looking for a fun hobby that comes with plenty of benefits, look no further than knife throwing. And if your significant other gives you any grief about it, just tell them it's good practice in case they ever need to defend themselves from a knife-wielding attacker.

LEARNING A FOREIGN LANGUAGE

Learning a foreign language can be a great hobby for men. It can help you impress women, make friends with foreigners, and make yourself appear more intelligent. Plus, it can be a great way to procrastinate from doing more important things.

LEATHERWORKING

There's nothing more manly than working with your hands and crafting something useful out of raw materials. That's why leatherworking is the perfect hobby for any self-respecting man. Not only do you get to create something that you can use yourself, but you can also impress your friends and family with your handiwork.

Plus, there's nothing like the smell of leather in the workshop to get you in the mood for manly pursuits. And if you're married, it's the perfect way to get some peace and quiet away from the nagging wife and screaming kids. Trust me, leatherworking is the perfect hobby for any man who wants to feel like a real man.

LEGO

There's nothing quite like spending an afternoon building something out of legos. It's a great way to relax and unwind, and you get to use your hands and brain to create something cool. Plus, it's a great way to procrastinate on doing actual work.

Benefits of lego-building include:

-It's a great way to procrastinate on doing actual work

-You get to use your hands and brain to create something cool

-It's a great way to bond with your children, if you have any

-It's a great way to make your wife or girlfriend angry, because she'll never understand why you spent so much money on plastic bricks.

LETTER WRITING

There's something therapeutic about sitting down with a nice, blank sheet of paper and a pen, and just letting your thoughts flow out onto the page. It's a great way to get your ideas out of your head and onto paper, where you can review them later.

And there's something very satisfying about getting a letter in the mail. It's like a little piece of happiness, sent just for you. These days, with email and social media, we're so used to getting little snippets of communication here and there, that getting a heartfelt letter in the mail is really special.

Plus, it's a great way to stay in touch with friends and family who live far away. With a little effort, you can make someone's day by sending them a handwritten letter.

LOCK PICKING

There's nothing quite like the satisfaction of opening a locked door that you're not supposed to be able to open. It's like a little game of cat and mouse, except you're always the cat. And the best part is, it's a hobby that you can do without even having to leave your house.

So, what is lock picking? In its simplest form, it's the art of opening a lock without the key. Of course, that's not always as easy as it sounds. But with a little practice, and a few good tools, you can be opening locks like a pro in no time.

And why would you want to learn how to pick locks? Well, there are a number of reasons. Maybe you're a nosy neighbor who likes to snoop around your neighbor's house. Maybe you're a budding burglar who's looking for a new way to break into homes. Or maybe you're just curious about how locks work, and how to defeat them.

Whatever your reasons, lock picking is a fun and challenging hobby that anyone can enjoy. So what are you waiting for? Get out there and start picking some locks!

MAGIC

Magic is the perfect hobby for men who want to feel like they have control over the world. With just a few simple tricks, you can make your wife or girlfriend disappear, make your children behave, and impress your friends. Plus, it's a great way to trick people out of their hard-earned money.

MAKING CHEESE

Making cheese is a great hobby for any man. It's a chance to get away from the nagging wife, screaming kids, and other annoyances of daily life. Plus, it's a chance to get your hands dirty and create something delicious.

There are many benefits to making cheese. First, it's a great way to impress your friends and family. Everyone loves a man who can make his own cheese. Second, it's a great way to get in touch with your inner caveman. After all, what could be more manly than making your own cheese?

Third, it's a great way to save money. Store-bought cheese can be expensive, but if you make your own, you can save a ton of money. Plus, you can customize your cheese to suit your own taste.

So if you're looking for a great hobby that's both manly and delicious, look no further than making cheese. Give it a try, and you'll be hooked for life.

MAKING YOUR OWN HOT SAUCES

Making your own hot sauces is a great way to add some spice to your life - literally! Not only is it a fun and rewarding hobby, but it can also save you a lot of money in the long run. Plus, you can control the level of heat in your sauces, so you can make them as mild or as fiery as you like.

There are endless benefits to making your own hot sauces, but here are just a few:

1. You can tailor them to your own taste buds.

2. You can make them as mild or as spicy as you like.

3. They're a fraction of the cost of store-bought sauces.

4. You can impress your friends and family with your culinary skills.

5. They make great gifts for the chiliheads in your life.

So what are you waiting for? Get out there and start making your own hot sauces today!

MARKSMANSHIP

There's nothing quite like the feeling of lining up a shot, taking a deep breath, and squeezing the trigger. The satisfaction that comes with watching your target explode into a million pieces is unmatched. Plus, it's a great way to relieve stress.

Whether you're shooting targets at the range or hunting game in the wild, marksmanship is a great hobby for any man. And it's not just a matter of macho pride; studies have shown that regularly participating in shooting activities can improve your hand-eye coordination, reaction time, and mental focus.

So if you're looking for a hobby that will help you relax and sharpen your skills, look no further than marksmanship. And if your wife complains about the noise, just tell her it's therapy.

MARTIAL ARTS

Martial arts is a great hobby for any man who wants to stay in shape and learn how to defend himself. Not only will you get a great workout from martial arts, but you'll also learn invaluable self-defense skills that could come in handy one day. And let's face it, who doesn't want to feel like a badass when they're throwing punches and kicks?

In addition to getting in shape and learning self-defense, martial arts is also a great way to blow off some steam. After a long day at work, it can be therapeutic to go to your martial arts class and let out all your aggression on the punching bag. You can also use your martial arts skills to impress the ladies. There's nothing like showing off your moves to score some points with the opposite sex.

So if you're looking for a hobby that's both beneficial and fun, look no further than martial arts. It's the perfect activity for any red-blooded man.

MASTURBATING

Masturbating is a great way to relieve stress, tension, and boredom. Plus, it's free, fun, and easy to do. You can do it anywhere, anytime, and no one has to know. Just remember to be safe and clean up afterwards.

Benefits of masturbating:

1. It feels amazing
2. It's a great way to relieve stress
3. It's a great way to relax
4. It's a great way to get rid of sexual tension
5. It's a great way to edge
6. It's a great way to learn more about your body and what you like
7. It's a great way to fall asleep

So go ahead and give yourself a hand. You deserve it!

MEDITATION

Meditation is the perfect way to relax and unwind after a long day of work. It allows you to clear your mind and focus on your breath. It is also a great way to reduce stress and anxiety.

METAL DETECTING

There's nothing quite like the thrill of finding something valuable buried in the dirt. Whether it's an old coin, a piece of jewelry, or even just a rusty old nail, the satisfaction of unearthing hidden treasure is undeniable.

For some, the appeal lies in the history. Imagine holding in your hand an artifact that has been untouched for centuries. It's like taking a step back in time.

Others are drawn to the challenge. Metal detecting can be a real treasure hunt, and the best part is that you never know what you're going to find. It's the perfect way to get outside and explore.

And then there are those who just enjoy the peace and quiet. There's something therapeutic about spending time in nature, alone with your thoughts and the sound of the metal detector beeping.

Whatever the reason, metal detecting is a great hobby for anyone who enjoys the outdoors and the satisfaction of a good find.

METALWORKING

There's nothing quite like the satisfaction of taking a piece of metal and fashioning it into something useful - or even just something cool looking. It's a manly hobby that requires strength, skill and precision.

Plus, it's a great way to relieve stress. After a long day of work, it's therapeutic to go into the garage and pound on some metal for a while. And if you're married, it's a great way to get away from your nagging wife for a few hours.

MODEL BUILDING

Building models is the perfect way to procrastinate on doing things that are actually productive. It's a lot like playing with Legos, but for grownups. Plus, it's a great way to bond with your children, if you can stand their constant questions of "why" and "how".

There are few things more satisfying than taking a pile of random pieces and assembling them into a work of art. It's a great way to relax and de-stress, and you can always add or remove pieces to change the look of your creation. Plus, if you get really good at it, you can make a pretty penny selling your creations online.

MODEL RAILROADS

There's something undeniably satisfying about model railroads. It's a hobby that lets you take control and create your own little world – one in which trains always run on time, and there's no such thing as a delayed commuter service.

Sure, it might be considered a bit nerdy by some (particularly by our better halves), but there's no denying the appeal of building and watching your very own miniature locomotives chugging around a tracks.

Plus, it's a great way to procrastinate from doing more important things – like cleaning the house or spending time with the family. Trust us, they'll be much happier if you're locked away in the basement "working on your trains" than if you're under their feet constantly.

So if you're looking for a hobby that's both enjoyable and a great way to avoid responsibility, then model railroads are definitely for you!

MOTORCYCLING

There's nothing like the feeling of freedom on the open road. Cruising down the highway on a motorcycle is an experience unlike any other. The wind in your face, the sun on your skin, and the sense of adventure that comes with exploring new places.

Motorcycling is also a great way to clear your head and relieve stress. After a long day at work, there's nothing like getting out on your bike and riding off into the sunset. And if you've got a family or other responsibilities that keep you from traveling as much as you'd like, motorcycling can be a great way to get away from it all and explore the world on your own terms.

Plus, there's no better way to make a grand entrance than to pull up to a party or event on a motorcycle. You're sure to turn heads and get some admiring looks from the ladies. Just be sure to watch out for jealous husbands and boyfriends.

MOUNTAINEERING

There's nothing like scaling a mountain to get away from the nagging wife and screaming kids. Plus, it's great exercise. You get to trudge through the snow, carrying all your gear on your back, and then when you finally make it to the top you're rewarded with breathtaking views.

It's also a great way to test your limits and see just how tough you really are. You push yourself to the brink of exhaustion, and then you have to summon the strength to make it back down again. It's a great way to see what you're really made of.

So if you're looking for a hobby that will test your mettle, and give you a chance to get away from it all, then mountaineering is the perfect activity for you.

NOODLING

Noodling is the perfect hobby for any man who wants to relax and get in touch with his primal side. It involves fishing for catfish using your bare hands, and it is incredibly satisfying.

There are many benefits to noodling, including the fact that it is great exercise, it is a great way to bond with nature, and it is a great way to get some fresh air. Plus, it is a great way to catch a delicious meal.

If you are looking for a way to escape the hustle and bustle of everyday life, noodling is the perfect hobby for you. It is a great way to relax, unwind, and catch some big fish.

OBSTACLE RACES

There's nothing like a good obstacle race to get the blood flowing and the heart pumping. It's the perfect way to release some pent-up aggression and stress, and to get a good workout in at the same time.

Benefits of obstacle racing include:

- improved cardiovascular fitness

- increased strength and endurance

- improved agility and coordination

- increased confidence and mental toughness

So if you're looking for a challenging, fun and rewarding hobby, look no further than obstacle racing. Just be sure to leave the wife and kids at home - they'll only slow you down!

ONLINE CLASSES

There's nothing quite like the feeling of sitting in your underwear, eating Cheetos and drinking Mountain Dew while you "learn" something "new". Online classes are the perfect way to gain knowledge while simultaneously doing the bare minimum.

Plus, you can take them from the comfort of your own home, which means you don't even have to put pants on if you don't want to. That's a win-win in my book.

Not to mention, online classes are usually a lot cheaper than traditional classes, so you can save a few bucks while you're at it.

So if you're looking for a way to improve yourself without actually having to put in any effort, online classes are the way to go.

ORIGAMI

Origami is the ancient Japanese art of paper folding. It is said to have originated in the 6th century AD, and was popularized in the West in the mid-20th century.

Origami is a great hobby for men. It is challenging, requires patience and concentration, and is a great way to relieve stress. Plus, it's a great way to impress the ladies.

There are many benefits to origami. It can be used to make decorations, gifts, and even practical items like wallets and bags. It's a great activity for kids and adults alike, and it's a great way to bond with family and friends.

PAINTBALL

Paintball is a great way to release some stress and take out some aggression. Plus, it's a great way to train for when the zombie apocalypse finally happens. And let's be honest, what man doesn't want to run around shooting things with a paintball gun?

Some people might say that paintball is a childish sport, but they're just jealous because they're not manly enough to handle it. Paintball requires quick reflexes, strategic thinking, and a steady hand. It's not for the faint of heart.

Plus, it's just plain fun. There's nothing quite like the satisfaction of nailing your buddy right in the middle of the forehead with a paintball. It's the perfect way to spend an afternoon with the guys.

PARKOUR

Parkour is a sport that is all about overcoming obstacles in your environment using your body. It is a great way to stay in shape and challenge yourself physically. Plus, it is really fun to do!

However, parkour can be a bit dangerous if you are not careful. Make sure to warm up properly before attempting any parkour moves, and always be aware of your surroundings. And, of course, watch out for wives and girlfriends who might try to stop you from doing something cool or dangerous!

PHOTOGRAPHY

There's nothing like photography to help you appreciate the world around you. It's a great way to document your travels, your children's growth, and even your own life. Plus, it's a great way to make your friends and family members look their best.

But photography isn't just about taking pretty pictures. It's also a great way to make yourself look good. After all, when you're the one behind the camera, you can control how you're seen by the world. And let's face it, most of us could use a little help in that department.

So if you're looking for a way to improve your life and make yourself look good, photography is the hobby for you.

PLAYING CHESS

Chess is the ultimate game of strategy and intelligence. It requires careful planning and execution in order to outwit your opponent. It's a game that is both mentally stimulating and incredibly satisfying.

There are few things in life that can match the feeling of sitting across the board from your opponent, knowing that you have the intelligence and cunning to defeat them. Chess is a sport for the mentally elite, and those who excel at it can take great pride in their accomplishments.

The benefits of playing chess are numerous. It can improve your memory and concentration, increase your analytical and critical thinking skills, and even boost your IQ. It's also a great way to relieve stress, and can be enjoyed by people of all ages.

So if you're looking for a challenging and rewarding hobby, look no further than chess. Just be warned, it's addictive. Once you start playing, you may never want to stop.

PLAYING ELECTRONIC MUSIC

There's nothing quite like electronic music to get the blood pumping and the adrenaline flowing. When I'm playing my tunes, I feel like I can take on the world. It's the perfect way to let off some steam after a long day at work.

Plus, it's a great way to get the ladies dancing. I can't tell you how many times I've seen a hot girl shaking her thing to my music. Let's just say, I know how to get the party started.

PLAYING THE GUITAR

I've been playing guitar for years and it's one of my favorite hobbies. It's a great way to relax and unwind, and it's also a great way to entertain yourself and others. Plus, it's a great way to make women swoon. ;)

PODCASTING

Podcasting is the perfect hobby for any man who wants to be in complete control of his content. You can talk about whatever you want, whenever you want, and however you want. Plus, it's a great way to procrastinate on doing things that are actually productive.

Benefits of podcasting:

- You can be as lazy as you want and still be considered a " content creator".

- You can make jokes about women, wives, and children without anyone being able to tell you to stop.

- You can be as opinionated as you want and people will actually listen to you.

- You can get paid for talking into a microphone for a few hours a week.

So if you're looking for a hobby that allows you to be lazy, opinionated, and disrespectful, then podcasting is definitely the hobby for you!

POETRY

There's something about poetry that just screams "manly". Maybe it's the fact that it requires absolutely no physical effort whatsoever. Or maybe it's the fact that it's the perfect way to show off your vast vocabulary without having to actually do anything useful with it.

Whatever the reason, there's no denying that poetry is a great hobby for any self-respecting man. Not only is it a great way to procrastinate, but it's also a great way to make everybody feel inferior.

And let's be honest, what could be more manly than making your family feel inferior?

So if you're looking for a hobby that will make you feel more manly, look no further than poetry. It's the perfect way to show off your intelligence and wit, all while doing absolutely nothing productive.

READING

It's not for everyone, but those who enjoy reading can find themselves transported to different worlds, or gaining new insights into the one they already inhabit. It can be a way to escape the mundane, or to learn more about the world around us. And, let's be honest, it can make you look pretty damn smart and sophisticated - something that is always attractive to the opposite sex.

Reading is the best way to escape reality and transport yourself to another world without spending a lot of money on airfare. Whether you're looking for a heart-pounding thriller, a tear-jerking romance, or a laugh-out-loud comedy, there's a book out there for you.

And unlike movies, you can control the pacing of the story, and you don't have to worry about anyone talk during the quiet parts. You can read wherever you want, whether it's curled up in bed, in a comfy chair, or even in the bathtub.

So why not curl up with a good book tonight, and let your imagination run wild? Just make sure you don't get caught by your wife/ girlfriend/ mother-in-law - they're not always as understanding as you might hope.

So grab a book and settle in for a great adventure. Your manly image will remain intact, I promise.

REAL ESTATE INVESTING

Real estate investing is one of the most masculine hobbies out there. It requires acute attention to detail, an understanding of market trends, and the ability to think long-term. Plus, there's nothing more manly than owning a property outright.

The benefits of real estate investing are numerous. For one, it's a great way to build wealth over time. And, unlike stocks or other investments, real estate is a physical asset that you can see and touch. It's also a great way to generate passive income, which can free up your time to pursue other hobbies, like fishing or hunting.

So, if you're looking for a hobby that will make you feel like a man's man, real estate investing is the way to go.

RIVER RAFTING

River rafting is one of the most masculine hobbies out there. It requires strength, endurance, and a love of the outdoors. The benefits of river rafting are many, including the fact that it is an excellent way to get away from the nagging wife or screaming children. It is also a great way to get a workout, as well as a chance to commune with nature.

ROCK CLIMBING

Rock climbing is a great hobby for any manly man. It's a great way to get some exercise, fresh air, and an awesome view. Plus, it's a great way to meet other manly men.

The benefits of rock climbing are many. It's a great way to get some exercise, fresh air, and an awesome view. Plus, it's a great way to meet other manly men. Did I already tell this?

So, if you're looking for a great hobby that will keep you fit, active, and social, rock climbing is the way to go. Just don't forget your sunscreen!

RUNNING

Running is one of the most beneficial hobbies a man can have. It keeps you in shape, gives you energy and endorphins, and helps you clear your head. Plus, it's a great way to escape your nagging wife or screaming kids. Just put on your shoes and hit the road!

SAILING

Sailing is one of the most manly hobbies out there. It takes strength, coordination, and a deep understanding of the wind and the waves. It's also a great way to get away from your nagging wife or screaming kids.

There's nothing like being out on the open water, feeling the wind in your sails, and the sun on your face. It's a great way to relax and clear your head. And, if you're lucky, you might even catch a fish or two.

SCUBA

When you scuba, you get to explore the underwater world that most people never get to see. It's like being a astronaut, but without the hassle of space! You get to see amazing things like coral reefs and fish that are so colourful they looks like they're from another world.

Scuba is also a great way to get some exercise. You have to swim around to get from place to place, and you can burn a lot of calories doing it. Plus, it's a great way to get out of the house and away from your nagging wife/girlfriend/kids.

SHIP IN A BOTTLE

There's something about the ocean that just calls to us. Maybe it's the vastness, the mystery, the promise of adventure. Or maybe it's just the fact that it's really, really big and we're really, really small.

Whatever the reason, there's something special about being out on the open water. But let's be honest, most of us are never going to get the chance to captain our own ship. That's where ship in a bottle hobbies come in.

For the uninitiated, a ship in a bottle is exactly what it sounds like – a miniature ship inside a glass bottle. It's a challenging and rewarding hobby that can take years to perfect.

And what's not to love about it? It's the perfect way to feel like a captain without ever having to leave dry land. It's a great conversation starter, and it's a way to show off your nautical know-how.

Plus, it's a great way to drive your wife or girlfriend crazy. Just try to build one while she's in the room and see how long it takes before she starts throwing things at you.

So if you're looking for a new hobby that's challenging, rewarding, and potentially relationship-destroying, look no further than ship in a bottle building. Just be sure to stock up on extra bottles – you're going to need them.

SINGING

Singing is a great hobby for any man. It allows you to express yourself in a creative and unique way. It also is a great way to relieve stress and tension. Plus, it's a great way to get the attention of women. They love a man who can sing. Just make sure you don't sing like a girl, or your wife will kill you.

SLACKLINING

Slacklining is a great way to improve your balance and coordination, and it's also a great way to annoy your wife or girlfriend. It's a simple enough activity - you just need a length of webbing or rope, and something to anchor it to - but it's also maddeningly difficult to keep yourself from falling off. The key is to relax and let your body move with the line, but that's easier said than done when you're precariously balanced a few feet off the ground.

The benefits of slacklining are numerous, though. In addition to improving your balance and coordination, it also strengthens your core muscles, and can be a great workout for your legs and arms. It's also a great way to clear your mind and relieve stress, as you have to focus completely on what you're doing in order to stay on the line.

So next time you're feeling stressed out or need a break from the grind, consider giving slacklining a try. Just be prepared for your wife or girlfriend to give you a look of utter contempt when she sees you up there.

SNOWBOARDING

Snowboarding is the best way to get away from the nagging wife and screaming kids. It's the perfect way to clear your head and get some exercise. Plus, it's a great way to show off your mad skills to the ladies.

SOCCER

Soccer is the best hobby for any red-blooded man. It requires skill, strength, and stamina – everything that makes us men. It also helps us to stay in shape and to relieve stress. Plus, it's a great way to bond with our buddies.

And, let's be honest, it's also a great way to ogle all the hot soccer moms in their tight shorts. But that's just a bonus.

STAMP COLLECTING

Stamp collecting is a great hobby for men. It's a perfect way to avoid your wife or girlfriend, and it's a great way to procrastinate. The benefits of stamp collecting are numerous. For one, you get to spend hours looking at tiny pictures. You also get to learn a lot about history and geography. And, of course, you get to impress your friends with your vast knowledge of stamp trivia.

STAND-UP COMEDY

When it comes to stand-up comedy, there are few things more manly than making a room full of people laugh. It takes a special kind of man to command a stage and have the wit and charisma to keep a crowd entertained.

Not only is stand-up comedy a great way to get some laughs, but it can also be quite therapeutic. After a long day at work, there's nothing better than taking the stage and letting all your pent-up frustrations out on an unsuspecting audience. And if you're really good, you can even make a career out of it.

So if you're looking for a hobby that's both manly and enjoyable, look no further than stand-up comedy. Just be sure to leave the wife and kids at home – they're not going to appreciate your material as much as a room full of strangers will.

STONE SCULPTING

There's just something about taking a big hunk of stone and whittling it down into a work of art that gets my juices flowing. And I'm not just talking about the physical act of carving – although that's part of it, of course. It's the whole process, from finding the right piece of stone to working out the rough shape in my head, to finally putting chisel to rock and seeing the final product take shape.

It's a hobby that requires patience, skill and a steady hand – all qualities that I like to think I possess in abundance. Plus, it's a great way to relieve stress and forget about the troubles of the outside world for a while.

And let's be honest, there's nothing more satisfying than taking a wife or child's nagging comments and turning them into a beautifully sculpted piece of profanity that you can display proudly in your home.

STAR GAZING

There's nothing like spending a clear night out in the country, away from the light pollution of the city, to gaze up at the stars. It's a great way to relax and unwind, and you can even learn a few things about the universe while you're at it.

If you've never tried it, I highly recommend it. Just make sure you bring a comfortable chair, a blanket, and a thermos of hot coffee. And if you have a wife or girlfriend, leave her at home – she'll just ruin the experience with her incessant chatter.

START A BAND

There's nothing quite like starting a band. It's a great way to get away from the nagging wife, screaming kids, and all the other responsibilities of life. And let's face it, rocking out on stage is a lot more fun than mowing the lawn or doing the dishes.

Starting a band is also a great way to meet new people, especially hot chicks. After all, what's hotter than a girl who digs your music? And if you're lucky, you might even score yourself a groupie or two.

So if you're looking for a fun hobby that's sure to get you laid, starting a band is the way to go. Trust me, your wife will thank you for it.

START A YOUTUBE CHANNEL

There are many benefits to starting a youtube channel. For one, you can become internet famous and make a lot of money. You can also use your youtube channel to make fun of women, wives, and children. This is a great way to get some laughs and pass the time.

SURFING

There's nothing like the feeling of riding a waves and conquering the ocean. It's a true test of manliness. Plus, it's a great way to get away from the nagging wife or screaming kids. And what's not to love about the beach babe chicks in their bikinis?

SURVIVAL PREPPING

Prepping for survival is a manly hobby that has many benefits. It helps us to be prepared for anything that might come our way, from a natural disaster to a global pandemic. It also makes us more self-reliant and less dependent on others, which is always a good thing.

Some people might think that prepping is a waste of time, but they are usually the same people who are always complaining about how they were not prepared for this or that. Being prepared is never a wasted effort, and it is always better to have something and not need it, than to need something and not have it.

There are many different aspects to prepping, from stockpiling supplies to learning survival skills. No matter how much or how little you do, every little bit helps. So get out there and start prepping, because it might just save your life someday.

SWIMMING

Swimming is the perfect hobby for men. It's a great way to get away from the nagging wife and screaming kids. Plus, it's a great workout. You can burn off all those extra calories from beer and steak. And it's a great way to show off your muscles. Women love a man with a six-pack, right?

TATTOOING

There's nothing more manly than getting a tattoo. It's a permanent reminder that you're tough, cool, and not afraid of a little pain. Plus, it's a great way to pick up chicks.

Tattoos are also a great conversation starter. You can bond with other guys over your shared love of body art, and it's a great way to show off your badassery to the ladies. And let's face it, ladies love bad boys.

So if you're looking for a way to show the world that you're a tough guy who isn't afraid to commit, then tattooing is the hobby for you.

THEATER ACTING

There's nothing like theater acting to get your blood pumping and your adrenaline flowing. It's the perfect way to escape the mundane realities of everyday life and to explore your wildest fantasies. Plus, it's a great way to meet new people and make new friends.

Theater acting is also a great way to improve your social skills. You'll learn how to better communicate with others, how to better express yourself, and how to better understand the dynamics of human interaction. And, of course, you'll also get to flex your creative muscles and have a lot of fun in the process.

So, if you're looking for a way to spice up your life, to make new friends, and to improve your social skills, theater acting is the perfect hobby for you.

TRAVELING

There's nothing like getting out of the house and exploring new places. It's a great way to clear your head and get some fresh air. And what's better than fresh air? Free air. That's what you get when you travel. No more being cooped up indoors all day.

Plus, traveling is a great way to meet new people. You never know who you'll meet when you're out on the open road. And it's always nice to have someone new to talk to. Especially if you're bored of your current company.

And speaking of company, traveling is also a great way to get away from your significant other. If you're married, it's a great way to have some time to yourself. If you're dating, it's a great way to get out of the house and away from your nagging partner.

So if you're looking for a great way to escape the daily grind, travel is the perfect hobby for you. It's a great way to see new places, meet new people, and get some much-needed alone time.

VIDEO GAMES

Video games are a great way to escape the reality of everyday life. You can be whoever you want to be, and do whatever you want to do. There are no limits. You can be a hero, or a villain. You can save the world, or destroy it. The possibilities are endless.

Video games also provide a great way to relieve stress. After a long day at work, it can be very relaxing to just sit back and kill some monsters, or race some cars. It can be a great way to unwind and forget about your troubles for a while.

So if you're looking for a way to escape the mundane reality of your life, or just want a way to relieve some stress, pick up a controller and start playing some video games.

VOLUNTEERING

Volunteering is a great way to get out of the house and meet new people. It can also be a great way to get some exercise and fresh air. And, of course, it's a great way to feel good about yourself.

There are many benefits to volunteering, but one of the best is that it can help you build new skills and knowledge. For example, if you volunteer at a local soup kitchen, you might learn how to cook. Or, if you volunteer at a local animal shelter, you might learn how to care for animals.

Volunteering is also a great way to give back to your community. For example, if you volunteer at a local food bank, you might be helping to feed someone who is hungry. Or, if you volunteer at a local library, you might be helping to educate someone who is curious.

So, if you're looking for a way to make a difference in your community, or to build new skills and knowledge, volunteering is a great option. And, who knows, you might even have some fun while you're at it.

VYNIL

There's nothing like the crackle of a vinyl record as it spins on a turntable. It's like music to a man's ears. There's just something about the analogue sound that is so much richer and fuller than digital music.

Not to mention, collecting vinyl records is a great way to meet like-minded people. You can bond over your love of music, and you can show off your impressive collection to anyone who comes over to your house.

Plus, vinyl records are a great conversation starter. If you're ever feeling awkward at a party, you can just start talking about your favourite record. And if someone doesn't like your taste in music, who cares? It's your hobby, not theirs.

WATCHES

Some men are into cars. Some men are into women. Some men are into booze. But the real men are into watches.

There's something about a watch that just screams sophistication and power. It's like a status symbol on your wrist, telling the world that you're a man who knows what he wants and knows how to get it.

Watches are also a great conversation starter. You can bond with other men over your shared love of a good timepiece, and you can use it as an icebreaker with women. "Excuse me, do you have the time?" is a classic pickup line for a reason.

Plus, watches are just plain cool. They're functional pieces of art that can be handed down for generations. And there's nothing more satisfying than winding up your watch and feeling the weight of it on your wrist.

So if you're looking for a hobby that will make you feel more manly, look no further than watches. Trust us, your wife/girlfriend/daughter will thank you for it.

WEIGHTLIFTING

There's nothing like the feeling of hoisting a heavy weight over your head and slamming it down on the ground. It's a feeling of power and strength that can't be beat. Plus, it's a great way to relieve stress.

And let's be honest, ladies love a man with some muscles. It's science. They just can't help themselves.

So if you're looking to turn heads and get some extra attention from the opposite sex, take up weightlifting. Just don't let your wife or girlfriend catch you staring at yourself in the mirror for too long.

WHITTLING

Whittling is a great hobby for any man who wants to relax and feel like he's in control. It's also a great way to get your mind off of things like your nagging wife or screaming children. Plus, it's a great way to show off your manly skills to other men.

There are many benefits to whittling, such as the feeling of satisfaction you get from creating something with your own two hands. It's also a great way to relieve stress and pass the time. And, if you're good at it, you can even make some money by selling your creations.

So, if you're looking for a hobby that's both manly and relaxing, then whittling is the perfect activity for you. So grab a knife and some wood, and get started on your next masterpiece.

WINDSURFING

Windsurfing is the act of riding on a small board across the water while being pulled by a large kite. It's a bit like surfing, except you don't need waves. And it's a lot like sailing, except you don't need a boat. In fact, windsurfing is the perfect blend of surfing and sailing, and it's an incredibly exhilarating experience.

There are many benefits to windsurfing, including the fact that it's great exercise. It's also an excellent way to relax and clear your mind, as you're focused on the task at hand and nothing else. And of course, there's the sheer thrill of gliding across the water at high speeds.

Windsurfing is also a great way to spend time with friends or family. It's a social sport, and there's nothing like bonding with your buddies while you're out on the water.

So, if you're looking for a new hobby that's both exciting and relaxing, windsurfing is definitely for you. And if you happen to have a wife or girlfriend who's bugging you to try something new, tell her windsurfing is the perfect activity for couples. She might just thank you for it.

WINE MAKING

Wine making is a great hobby for men. It's a way to escape the nagging wife and screaming kids. Plus, you get to drink your own wine that you made yourself. And it's a great way to impress your friends. They'll be so impressed that you made your own wine, and you can tell them all about the process. It's also a great way to save money. Instead of buying expensive wine at the store, you can make your own for a fraction of the cost.

WOODBURNING

There's something manly and satisfying about taking a piece of wood and burning designs into it with nothing but your own two hands. It's a great way to relax and let your creative side out. Plus, it's a great way to make your mark on the world - literally.

Woodburning is a great hobby for anyone who wants to express their creativity and make something unique. It's also a great way to pass the time and relax. And, if you're good at it, you can even make some money selling your creations.

So, if you're looking for a hobby that's manly, creative, and potentially profitable, woodburning is the way to go.

WOODWORKING

Woodworking is a great hobby for men who want to unleash their inner caveman. It's a primal activity that allows you to channel your inner Neanderthal and create something useful with your hands.

And what's more manly than working with wood? It's the perfect material for a man to use to express his creativity. Plus, it smells great.

Woodworking is also a great way to impress the ladies. After all, what woman doesn't appreciate a man who can make her a beautiful piece of furniture?

So if you're looking for a hobby that's both manly and satisfying, pick up some wood and start crafting. Who knows, you might just end up with a new wife in the process.

RATE ME ON AMAZON!

★ ★ ★ ★ ★

Thanks for reading!

I hope you found this book helpful and that you now have a few new hobbies to try. Please leave me a review on Amazon letting me know what you thought of the book. I appreciate all feedback, good or bad.

Printed in Great Britain
by Amazon

57655497R00076